Query

What would it be like to touch you
in unfamiliar ways,

to let my body swim
into yours?
Your hand strokes

the fine soft hair on my cheek,
skimming my face.

I take in all the breath I can.

You have with me
the way of light with water.

How deep can you go?
How much can I hold?

What can we both keep after dark?

(page 16)

Each Hand A Map

by Anita Skeen

introduction by Eloise Klein Healy

the NAIAD PRESS inc.

1986

Printed in the United States of America
First Edition

Cover design by Tee Corinne
Typesetting by Sandi Stancil

The epigraph heading the poem "Topography" is used with permission of the artist, Debbie
Drechsler.

The opening epigraph "Because One Is Always Forgotten" from *The Country Between Us,* by
Carolyn Forche is used with the permission of the author.

The epigraph heading the poem "Ritual: Downtown Bar" from *Diving Deep and Surfacing:
Women Writers On Spiritual Quest,* by Carol P. Christ is used with the permission of the author
and the publisher, Beacon Press, 1980, 2nd Ed., 1986.

The epigraph heading the poem "Trimming The Tree" is reprinted from *Among Women* by
Louise Bernikow, Copyright 1980 by Louise Bernikow. Used with permission of the author
and the publisher, Harmony Books, a division of Crown Publishers, Inc.

The line from "Coast To Coast" from *A Wild Patience Has Taken Me This Far, Poems 1978-
1981,* by Adrienne Rich is used with the permission of the author and the publisher, W. W.
Norton, Inc., Copyright 1981 by Adrienne Rich.

The epigraph heading the poem "Somewhere Just Beyond" from "Voices From The Forest"
(in *The Need to Hold Still*), by Lisel Mueller is used with the permission of the author and the
publisher, Juniper Press, Copyright 1971 by Lisel Mueller.

The epigraph heading the poem "Naming" is from *When God Was A Woman,* by Merlin Stone,
originally published by Virago Press, 1976 with the title, *The Paradise Papers.* Published in the
U.S. by Harcourt, Brace Jovanovich, in conjunction with Dial Press.

Library of Congress Cataloging-in-Publication Data

Skeen, Anita.
    Each hand a map.

    1. Lesbians–Poetry.   I. Title.
PS3569.K374E2 1986   811'.54   86-12780
ISBN 0-930044-82-7

ACKNOWLEDGEMENTS

Acknowledgement is made to the following publications for poems that originally appeared in them:

Arrangement (Scott, Foresman) "Letter To My Mother"

Confluence: Contemporary Kansas Writers (Cottonwood Press): "How We Drive Each Other"

I Hear My Sisters Saying (Crowell & Sons) "Letter To My Mother"

Kansas Quarterly: "Driving Through Kansas, Eating a Pear"

New Letters: "The Back Fence"

Nimrod: "The Last Link"

Prairie Schooner: "Theory of Evolution" and "Lesson"

Thirteen: "Gift"

13th Moon: "City Park: March Sunday"

Woman Poet: The Midwest: "For Susan, Turning Thirty"

Yellow Silk: "Without Words"

for Beth,
who makes all things possible

I wish to express my thanks to the faculty and students of the Center for Women's Studies at Wichita State University for their continued support and appreciation of my work

and to Margaret Atwood, Carolyn Forche, and Adrienne Rich for their words and lives.

BIOGRAPHY

Anita Skeen was born in 1946 and grew up outside of Big Chimney, West Virginia. She brought dogs into her house, took books into the woods, and filled her childhood with an assortment of girls who were interested in everything from Davey Crockett to paper dolls to basketball. She graduated from Concord College in Athens, West Virginia, where she joined Sigma Sigma Sigma sorority to become captain of its intramural team and changed her major from physical education to English because of a professor who could teach poetry without using notes. She earned her graduate degrees from Bowling Green State University in Bowling Green, Ohio.

Her alliance with women is obvious in her teaching, her writing, her day-to-day existence. Her teaching and writing have been the leavening through which many women have risen to discover their strengths and their skills.

As she travels in her writing through experiences common to women's lives, she also travels geographically. Images and landscape shift and vary as widely as the stories she tells. Her writing reflects her appetite for new flavors of experience. More than once she has been overheard to remark, "Anything is worth it, if you have a good story to tell afterwards."

Anita Skeen is currently Associate Professor of English at Wichita State University in Wichita, Kansas where she teaches in the Creative Writing and Women's Studies Programs. She lives in a family composed of two women, two teenage boys, two dogs, two cats, and two rabbits.

CONTENTS

INTRODUCTION

It truly is an auspicious event that Naiad Press, for the first time, is publishing the work of a contemporary poet. The audience for women's poetry is diverse and deep, and in the choice of Anita Skeen's *Each Hand A Map* Naiad is presenting the work of a poet who is mature in her technical strengths and certain of her voice. Naiad Press has consistently and doggedly kept lesbian writing in public consciousness, and Skeen's work positively advances the way lesbian poetry examines women's lives and relationships.

This is not poetry obsessed with the drama of falling in/falling out of love. Although there are poems about love—about the beginnings and endings of love—the focus here is not on romance. Instead, the poetry is about all the facets of women's relationships with other women, particularly what we term friendship, though friendship is not a precise enough word for the various states Skeen writes of— states women are now beginning to examine with a keen consciousness of their historical antecedents and the new ways in which these relationships work in us.

There is a calm and considered tone in this work, as pacific as the color blue which appears often enough in this poetry to be viewed as a motif. This is work that compares to watercolor, showing in its lines ample proof of years of learning of craft, of language usage that is deft and to the point, and above all, of concerns not muddied by overstatement.

Much is asked of women's poetry in our time. The feminist movement has been fueled by its poets who have posed the questions we all need to come to terms with in our lives. Lesbian poets, certainly, have been in the forefront of those asking that we see with new eyes, hear new voices. Our poets have functioned as consciences and seers, their language filling in like small seedlings a terrain where nothing grew before. Plantings of all kinds have sprung from our poets, and we live in a time in which the gardens have asked more of the flowers than their beauty.

What a poet chooses to write about, though, cannot be the only thing that determines the value of the poem. The manner the poet employs also *is* the poem. When the manner and the matter can be spoken of as one, then we're talking about a poetry that can substantially reach our souls and minds interactively—a poetry that can show us how *we* are put together by how *it* is put together.

xv

Because our poetry has meant so much to our lives, a narrow focus on just form or just content makes for a meaningless academic trivialization of what the real relationship between subject, language, poet and reader is all about. That focus amidst only of seeing poetry as a kind of algebra, trapping us in talk about how the form fits the subject or if the topic is "correct." These ways of discussing poetry can never go far enough. How the form and the subject fit the object of the poem is another and more productive question to ask because then the reader and the poet both have to be figured into the equation. Then the real questions about poetry can leap out. What does the poetry demand that I do or allow me to think and feel? Just how does the poetry make me interact with it? A good question that at once has nothing to do with content and yet everything to do with content. As Gandhi said, "The means are the end in the making."

All this applies directly to Anita Skeen's work because not only do her subjects point us toward certain considerations, but her means of presenting her subjects tell us quite clearly how to think about them. We could say these poems give us the speed at which to play them, probably a good clue to the speed at which these incidents and emotions were lived, as well.

I think the best poetry of our time tells us how fast or how slow the perceptions or reactions from the poetry are to emerge. Everything in Skeen's work says to slow down, take time.

"Topography," the opening poem which also introduces us to the concept of "map," shows us a picture inside a picture—women sitting at tables drinking tea and talking. Two pictures. One is framed and hanging on the wall above the two women the poet focuses on. Skeen's presentation suggests "look more than once." She cautions "look often to find all the information that's there." With this poem, Skeen sets up what the book is about and how we are to learn this.

Like the map in the book's title, Skeen's poems can be seen as having two purposes. They can be used to chart unknown territory, or they can provide a history of the present moment, functioning like a map which shows us how the poet got to this point. It is the deliberateness of Skeen's work that counts so much, the consciousness in her poetry of the steps that have to be taken to get to places with people. Skeen's work is very sure in its desire to stand and speak forth even though the words she is saying (or the woman that she is) could bring down punishment on her, as she shows in "Theory of Evolution."

In this room all women wear left hands.
Our scissors are forged for someone
else, doors open on the wrong side, elbows
collide at the table. We are the awkward,
the maladroit. The sinister and the unlucky.

xvi

We work in the shadow of the descending ruler,
our teeth clenched, our knuckles tense
for the blow, and with that other hand, left
unguarded, we are articulating our first
words, leaning to touch
our new toes.

It is true, too, that the way you get anywhere touches and shapes you. Skeen's poetry catalogs the many ways women move each other or move with each other. For example, her friends and lovers drive her with words to words ("Elements" and "How We Drive Each Other"). In "Just Like In The Movies," small tokens and small gestures represent the years of connectedness. Neighborly concern is expressed by women with gifts of food at the death of a relative or loved one. "Women Who Cook" was one of my favorite poems about the simplest touching. My childhood memories of women in the little Iowa town I grew up in were awakened by this poem about women who express their compassion and sorrow through their cooking, emotion welling up in some tangible, edible form—some cookies, a pie, a ham.

A couple who read their guests' palms for a hobby told me that each palm has a different function. One shows what you were born with and the other reveals what you've made of yourself. They kept copies of all their visitors' palms in a big book and at each subsequent visit, they would reexamine the "doing" palm for changes. I was reminded of this when I read Skeen's poetry because there is such recognition in her poems that we work with givens. This is best shown in her poems dealing with long-term friendships.

"For Susan Turning Thirty" is one such poem. Very subtly it touches on differences in two women's lives, and in an almost imperceptible turn of phrasing, Skeen writes

. . .Now we are differences:
our choice of partners, the way
we dress, the books that change
our lives. I could not write this poem
for myself, I turned thirty
in September. Once again,
it is for you, it is for me.

The important word to me is "are"—"now we *are* differences," not that now we *have* differences. Friends of such duration remain friends, implies Skeen, because of the respect for what is not the same in them. The friendship is formed time and time again regardless of the differences they "are." What is the given is what one creates out of.

The poems in this collection have a strong narrative character. Poems of direct address in which a story is recounted dominate the book and give a feeling of frequent and meticulous reflection. I felt history always underfoot and the weight of what had gone before in relationships. Some few poems like "Query" create a surprise by contrast because they are achieved with quick strokes. But overall, Skeen's poems unveil themselves slowly and deliberately, detail after detail. Some of them tease and make great fun of doling out their information. "Mowing" is like that. So is "City Park: March Sunday," a favorite of mine because it is about softball and sports is a topic you don't see much about in poetry. In real life, however, sports and games are rituals many women share, and to touch on a team sport in light of its "tribal" and ritualistic aspects is a valuable contribution.

Skeen's poetry suggests that if you put yourself up against the world or another person, there are signs to be read, if you can first admit how large and telling even the smallest event in life is. This has been poetry's age old task, glimpsing, as Blake did, the universe in a grain of sand. In Skeen's work, this reading of signs often unfolds in her hands. As she touched something of the world, she is given an image of where she is on the psychical map.

A pair of poems, each expressing different states of feeling, start their lessons out in the palm of the hand.

The light on my hands, this late
afternoon, fills the cracks, the lines,
warms the fields of my palms. I turn
my hands down, remembering their shape
as they cradle your face, curve them up again,

dip them down in the sea. Water pours
out, leaving flecks of salt, weightless
as feathers, ghosts of the waves.
My hand is a white shell.
I study the curves.

—"Lesson"

The same hands can render a different message by what they touch as we see in "Phone Call."

Here in the cornfields
the stubble turns brittle
and shrunken leaves cling
to the trees despite rain.
When I hold their translucent skins
to the light, the veins lengthen

xviii

toward the edges in chaotic ways.
I press the leaf to my palm.
The lines coincide.

—"Phone Call"

A constellation of the images of hands, light and water figure in many of the poems. In "Query" the poet is asking the meaning of the sign because it is not clear in the meeting between the women.

You have with me
the way of light with water.

How deep can you go?
How much can I hold?

The next step in this line of inquiry is to admit there's more going on than even the poet's imagery can carry.

I would ring you now, bound for Eustis,
ask you to consider how our lives return
to us in unexpected ways, how it is
not our hands which hold
what matters most.

—"Driving Through Kansas, Eating A Pear"

In a poem whose title is also the first line, "These faded blue," the recurring images of the color blue, the light and the poet's hands all line up again, and once again the interaction of these three motifs create the reaction of the poet to her circumstances. "Writing In The House Where Everyone Sleeps" makes another use of the same grouping, as does "Gifts." Skeen's use of this triad reveals her skills in composing many different poems all based on the same small set of images. The strong underlying knit of the book leaps out if one pays attention to this single thread. The closing poem, "The Hands Of Women," spins the same circle and actually picks up key works from the entire collection to complete the various themes of relationship which run through the work.

Characteristically, Skeen doesn't encapsulate the major themes in only one poem. "Trimming The Tree" is also about the handclasps of friends, lovers and family across time and distance. In an entirely different style than that of the closing poem, Skeen goes back to her basic premise—everything that matters is life-long. In being honest with ourselves and our "others" we have to admit the complexity of parallel lines. In the long run, in the genuine grace of friendship and love, we may be brought to say to the women of our lives

... Alone with you
in this room tonight, I share
what centuries of women too often leave unsaid.
You give me gifts that need no wrap, no reasons.

—"Trimming The Tree"

Like many of us living in the white flurry of events at the end of this century, I often need to slow down, to find something solid, to get a clear fix on what life is all about. Having the opportunity to write about this collection of poems has been more of a blessing than I could have imagined or predicted. For my task I had to take some extra time to be with these poems, to turn them over in my own hands until I knew them as if they were really hands themselves. To be quite truthful, I needed this book for my life, and I am very grateful to Anita Skeen and to Naiad Press for the gift.

Eloise Klein Healy
Los Angeles, June 1986

The heart is the toughest part of the body.
Tenderness is in the hands.

Carolyn Forche

"Because One Is Always Forgotten"
The Country Between Us

to get to know the map

Topography

But it is the same land
And I begin to get to know the map
And to get my bearings.

—Dag Hammarskjold in a drawing by
Debbie Dreschsler.

Beneath the drawing, framed, hanging
On the panelled wall, we sit with tea
and lunch. In the picture, two women
bend toward each other across a wood table.
All this is done in blue ink.
One holds a white cup, blue stripe
orbiting the rim, steam rising in cryptic
clouds toward her face. She gestures
in response. The other, a cigarette
tottering in her right hand, listens
with tired eyes wide as the window behind them
which reveals a tree, ghost-grey
in the morning light. They are clothed
in robes. A slipper dangles from one
toe. Their hair, untouched
by wind, hangs uncombed.

I watch you dunk the teabag in your cup,
up and down, pull it tight to the side,
slide it to the glass plate. Not a drop
spots the blue-checked cloth.
You tell me that once everything you owned
was blue. I lift my cup, an old beer mug
filled now with iced tea, and look away
toward the window where the sky springs
blue as iris and the cedars rock
exhausted in the wind. I turn back
to the quiet room, to where you
say how with practice we learn,

3

how we repeat what we know again
and again. Your hands imitate a child
taking her first steps and I watch your eyes
thinking how light surprises me always,
how intimate it remains.

Lesson

I have spent the summer watching
the sea. Watching the streamlined gulls
dip in regular as the white tide.
Watching them dip out again.
Learning about curves.

Now your voice spills onto my shore
like the waves. It churns
over the smooth glass tunnel of green,
floods to places I do not expect.
I try to follow the curves.

You are the bird, too distant
to name, I try not to lose
sight of, a single wave
washing the sky. Light bends
from the curve of your wing.

The light on my hands, this late
afternoon, fills the cracks, the lines,
warms the fields of my palms. I turn
my hands down, remembering their shape
as they cradle your face, curve them up again,

dip them down in the sea. Water pours
out, leaving flecks of salt, weightless
as feathers, ghosts of the waves.
My hand is a white shell.
I study the curves.

Survival Poem

for Mary and Marianne

Two women inhabit these few rooms
constructing neighborhoods
of dishes, books, and fabric.
Their lives lie scattered
everywhere. They have tossed out secrets
with the trash, pushed back the limits
of their thought. They mention
friends at home, go occasionally
for mail, try to fall in love
with men who never write. I come here
to be off the streets, to sleep
where it is warm. I hang on
like a turtle to all that I can.

I go with them late to the ocean,
its dark tide bringing us another
night. Its animal softness
absorbs us as we build the fire, cook food,
rename the things we feel.

I drive home to search for sleep
on the five a.m. streets of this beach city.
Flutes of light spread out
across the sky, fingers stretching
for me. I reach back.

I dream we sit at the round table
together, as we often do, enough time
spread out before us like a feast.
We tell how we are the heroines
of each others' lives, the women
whose words lift us out of deep caves,

whose work is our work, whose grief
we store up with our own.
Light comes into my small room.
We stand embracing.

Naming

At the very dawn of religion, God
was a woman. Do you remember?

—Merlin Stone

1.
I sit at my desk to grade papers.
The red ink coils around the misspelled
words, the notebook holes, trails
the thin blue lines. The room
changes: I carve clay tablets,
a stylus in hand.
I record strange figures
on the rough surface. Gold and bronze
rings dress my hands. Serpents
encircle each limb. I write
my name, my mother's name,
my grandmother's name.
This is as far back
as I have been told.
It is not as far back as
I know.

2.
In this large fine house we make love.
Candles burn—vanilla, spruce,
jasmine. I push open
the darkness and dive in
to a temple full
of holy women. Women embracing,
women chanting, women singing.
None is silent.
They teach each other
sacred verses of love, the power
of dreams, the beauty of body.

They are priestess, prophet,
oracle. I cannot speak
their language, but I know
what they say.

3.
We have been lined up at this conference
table for hours. I will not give up
my place. The men reach to the inside
pockets of their three-piece suits,
draw out arrows. From their briefcases
they assemble bows, slings,
dump out stones. They are aiming
at me. I fight rather
than die. They call me unnatural
woman, Amazon, lesbian,
whore. I call to my sisters
for strength. I know
they will come.

4.
My house is protected by trees.
In the back an apple, at the side,
sycamore. No fig. No mulberry.
It is fall and the leaves light up
like dragon's breath.
I bite into the apple, a hard red
Jonathan, hear the crunch
of witches' bones cracking
on the rack, mothers' bones
breaking beneath a storm
of stones, daughters' bones
snapping in some man's grasp.
Such sin deserves just punishment.
Who the guilty are
we know.

Letter to my Mother

I remember when a Sunday friend and I,
bored with the good words of the morning and
the pleasantries of the noon meal,
escaped to the vacant lot behind our house
to play in the tall goldenrod
and, hidden in the top branches of the persimmon tree,
antagonize small children
unable to catch hold of the lower limbs.

How we teased obnoxious Stevie Bull,
spit on him with sing-song poems
and ripe orange persimmons
till he ran screaming through the weeds
a rodent harrassed by the jays,
into the nest of his old stone house.

How, seconds later, his mother
erupted through the screen door, arms flailing,
eyes ripping leaves from the top of the trees,
her voice frenzied and crackling
with promises of retribution
more immediate and terrible
than those threats of eternal damnation
we had absorbed nonchalantly a few hours before.
I still feel her words crash
through the soft sunlight,
shatter the colors of the warm afternoon
and scatter the laughter like dry leaves in a storm.

How I dropped hard to the ground,
my heart banging against my ears, bursting
through the last tangled minutes onto the front porch,
each stride bringing nearer the ring
of the phone,

each breath adding
new lines to my story.

I do not remember what she said when she called,
what I said in defense or what
you said at all
and though there will be no more
angry mothers, no more Sunday games,
no more teasing of innocence
sometimes in still moments
that autumn terror
returns
leaves me stunned,
breathless,
naked in the garden
and I hear the steady ringing of the phone
into the long night.

Theory of Evolution

*for Diane Lewis, Celia Traugh,
Cathy Burack, and others*

You were the first
they did not try to change. They let you
do it your way, knowing all along
that it was the wrong side of your brain
in control, but resisting the constant urge
to slap that wooden ruler across your plump
white hand. One, in fact, about fifth grade,
even encouraged your efforts
at penmanship, despite your handicap.
Adoringly you returned at lunch
and after school to stand, web-footed,
for hours before the black slate
carving symbols to music. For the marches,
there were rows and rows of *h* and *k* and *b*.
m, n, and assorted vowels waltzed
their way into your vocabulary. You worked
hard, you were rewarded: a trip to
a teachers' meeting where your hand,
uncriticized, but, of course, not unnoticed,
danced shamelessly before the eyes of scholars.
So used to those fluid movements, those halts
and starts, the Masters battling
in your skull, in sleep you wore out
rooms of blackboards, cases of chalk, the letters growing
louder on each line, tentacles of language squeezing
you through the gritty floorboards. Awake, you dreamed
of becoming Miss America, of winning the talent
competition hands down.

In this room all women wear left hands.
Our scissors are forged for someone

else, doors open on the wrong side, elbows
collide at the table. We are the awkward,
the maladroit. The sinister and the unlucky.
We work in the shadow of the descending ruler,
our teeth clenched, our knuckles tense
for the blow, and with that other hand, left
unguarded, we are articulating our first
words, learning to touch
our new toes.

Wanting Some Other Sign

All night my body swims
among fevers
your face often the white fish
I trail

hoping for some clue
I suspect words
in the murmur of grasses
I pass through, history

unclaimed in the caves below
Your face ascends
on white wings
a twig of green dropped

at the door of my midnight ark
Beneath the sheets my arms
arch, a rainbow
of nerves, my radar in dreams

Outside the stars
strut forth like poppies
their stems streaming, tails
of comets or late December

fire, like lanterns
bobbing in the old North Church tower
I study the spokes
of light wheeling on water

A single white fish flashes through
leaves strange language
tangled like seaweed
across the walls of my sleep

Phone Call

Your voice reaches me
this cold October night like an ember
popping from the fire or the wind
sudden around the corner
of this metal trailer. My breath catches:
a leaf scuttles like a squirrel
across the bend in the road.
I expected it would be different
after so long.

I have seen you all month
in the shells of delicate purple
I searched for along
miles of white sand,
in the unpredictability
of sunsets, and later, in the blood
and gold coins of the autumn woods.
As I come farther north,
you come nearer.

Here in the cornfields
the stubble turns brittle
and shrunken leaves cling
to the trees despite rain.
When I hold their translucent skins
to the light, the veins lengthen
toward the edges in chaotic ways.
I press the leaf to my palm.
The lines coincide.

Query

What would it be like to touch you
in unfamiliar ways,

to let my body swim
into yours?
Your hand strokes

the fine soft hair on my cheek,
skimming my face.

I take in all the breath I can.

You have with me
the way of light with water.

How deep can you go?
How much can I hold?

What can we both keep after dark?

Rumor

I knew then I should've walked home but they insisted
so I said *yes* and we hurried through the dark
parking lot lights abandoning us on each side and
I asked about Space Invaders and one said she had hit
17,000 and would soon be like the boy whose friends
had to stuff sandwiches in his mouth while he played
and I told about my cold and then said *what's new
in town* and they told me as I climbed in the back
seat the door snapping too fast behind me not even
feeling the frozen teeth of the seat as I said *oh
who is it* and they looked at each other while my heart
spread out into my whole body and finally one said
and then getting home by 10:00 wasn't a problem and
I said *how'd you know* and one said it came from
a reliable source someone I myself knew had never
spread a word of gossip someone who would say nothing
rather than something bad and I felt myself slipping
deeper into the mouth of the back seat and my hands
had to grab for something which turned out to be
my books and we pulled up by my house and someone
said *which door* and I said *she plays tennis too*
and we turned down the side street and stopped
at the curb with the engine running and I saw
my porch light and I said I might go to Kansas City
but I wasn't sure yet I had to call and check the date
I wasn't the one getting tickets but now it might be
different you could never tell I was shocked
but not surprised they'd been such good friends
all fall and the last time we had pizza they shared
one but so did lots of other people and I felt
my fingers burn on the handle of the door as
it swung open and I stepped out into the stiff wind
and said *thanks goodnight*

17

Driving Through Kansas, Eating A Pear

I squeeze the cold sweetness
of this breast-like fruit
between my tongue and teeth
and recall the two of us
stealing fruit one Sunday afternoon,
me coiling around the limb
like that first snake, tossing you,
solid on the earth below,
the small green pears.

The fields I cross now
are tossed with green,
their golden wheat an early summer
blessing, even though this year
it's half the size.
Combines work the fields
cutting paths (Moses
parting the Red Sea, I think
you would say), walls weaving upright
on both sides.

I think of you, also crossing Kansas today,
headed north through Nebraska in your own car,
each of us leaving our midwest lives
for a time.
The telephone poles string out
as far as I can see, crosses
that will bear our voices state to state.
I would ring you now, bound for Eustis,
ask you to consider how our lives return
to us in unexpected ways, how it is
not our hands which hold
what matters most.

Over Breakfast

in the middle of my scrambled eggs,
you ask the question
I have been thinking for days:
How are you feeling
about this relationship as it now stands?
My fork spears a finger
on my left hand as my interest
in hash browns becomes clinical.
All I know how to do is grin
when I look at you,
unwinding your cinnamon roll
like an ace bandage.
You are grinning, too.
Positive, I say
as I feel my body wired
with electric shock, my knife
a chain saw shredding
the bread. I press potatoes
and eggs into a long soft wall
between us, recalling something
about fences and good neighbors.
Answering questions clearly
is a skill I never learned.
I tried for gymnastics instead.
Can I cartwheel my way through?
I am already tripping the balance beam.
Uneven parallels are next.
In this tiny diner,
already crowded before eight,
the waitress spins
from booth to booth
like a song on the wrong speed.
As she rotates by, you ask
only for more coffee.

I am wanting more words,
not those on the menu or those she trusts
for explanation as she matches
the square corners of her wet rag,
but words, like the fruit
of still life, luscious
and permanent at the same time.

Without Words

You lie naked on this white float
in the pool, the bleached print
from your swimsuit exposed
to the burn of the afternoon
sun. I spill oil on the unprotected
skin, my fingers linking slow
circles around your breast, diagonals
from the breast to rib, straight line
along your leg. I watch
the water inch around you, rise
in the indentations on the raft, see
it under you like a liquid sheet,
between your thighs like my moving hand.
My hand, a tin cup, dips in.

Returning Home

You sleep at night
your back toward me

your outline
indistinct, that first vague rim
of Colorado mountains

a day's drive west of here

Years ago I lived
in mountains
found them intimate

when autumn
flecked the trees
with such peculiar light

When snow came
I still sought the caves
of their limbs
bundled, clumsy as a bear
in all the clothes
I owned

rather than cluster
by the wood stove
with the rest

Once when I came back
my feet were packed in ice

like frail bones
of something extinct

They dug me from the red boots

Now those mountains
they tell me are stitched

with interstates and shopping malls
crop out like veins of coal

I can't go back
When you leave for work

in the morning, the horizon
stretches out flat

as my arms, extended
wanting embrace

an unmarked detour

Women in Doorways

1.
We begin in doorways, our journey through water,
our passage complete. From here all paths
are departures. We wake in the middle
of narratives, waiting for a way in,
a way out of the plot. Intermission
comes at the wrong time. We leave parents,
hometowns, husbands. Mostly we leave
women: mothers, sisters, roommates, best friends.
We leave room, turn inward for access.

I stand at the iron gate in summer shirt sleeves
waving, metronome-like, to the green Ford
dissolving in gravel and dust. From the window,
she waves back: I hold the cracker jacks
with no prize. I have missed the last bus home.

In the arch of a church, a daughter
leaves the arm of one man,
catches another like a gold ring.
The lens of my camera cracks.
Her face turns toward mine, its cameo
pinned forever to my throat.
I swing for a moment, a loose hinge,
one screw lost.

Outside, I take an unmarked
detour, walk the street, a dry canal,
its white stripes buoys in the dark.

2.
We meet in the dooryard outside
a Japanese cafe. I am coming out.

You are coming in. Early imprints
hold us a long time.

I arrive from Portland, an hour away.
You open the screen door,
wrap me in an unexpected hug.
I stay dressed in the shape of your arms
for days.

I lie in bed, ready
to turn out the light.
You arch in the doorway,
a silky rainbow.
You talk, stand there longer
than I ever knew
I could hold my breath.

We lie, not sleeping, in my bed.
Talk worries the night.
You get up, head out
of the room. I see you
framed by bathroom light,
your body a song
I am trying to learn.

I linger in your office.
You work at the desk.
I have run through my list
and have to leave.
I am caught in the doorway,
hooked on the line
of your voice.

Summer night clings
to the screen, a honeycomb
of hot air. I watch you
walk to your car, wait

for the scrape of the engine,
the surprise of lights.
I watch till the street
empties, till the leaves
in the gutters drown
under deep snow.

3.
Here she stands to tell me goodnight,
to flip out the light, where she stands

at 6:00 a.m. flipping it on again, to wake me
for school. She will not be at the front door

when I leave, still in the dark, or when I return.
She will be at a downtown office, knocking

on the lawyer's door, asking about the deposition
she has just typed. Her mother waits

in the doorway outside. They are both younger
than I ever recall. They leave, walk up

Summers Street past the women lolling in doorways
of the Rialto Theater, the Murphy Hotel.

They avoid the photograph faces,
pray silently for the resurrection

of us all. They board the bus, wedged
in the door against shoppers, office workers,

as they drop coins in the glass case.
On the ride home they talk of cupboards,

bank books, the weekend wedding.
The bus stops. They get off and climb

the steep road home in the grey evening light.
The doorbell rings. The door opens.

They wash in with the dark air.
We bob together at the threshold,

lighting the channels between us,
bells breaking the surface of the night.

Travelers

In the belly of the clouds, the storm
wakes from hibernation. We wait

indoors drinking coffee at square tables,
watching the flight of hands at cards.

We grasp words like rungs
on a crude ladder. Outside

the landscape sits
as if abandoned.

A windmill glows bronze
as a sacred staff in the electric sky.

Back in the Suppesville Cafe,
we struggle through caves and corridors

of our own design, some of us in silence,
some on horseback, others in fancy evening dress,

troubled by visions of pumpkins and mice.
The screen door flaps periodically

against the warped frame, interrupting
nothing. I watch shadows fold loose

on the face of the woman alone
in the front booth. She raises her cup

towards me. We balance
on each end of a long breath.

The Last Link

This ring I wear is not
a circle, the emblem of the sun
Perfection died with the old Greeks
Eternity is the time I spend
knowing where you are
This ring is a square, a foundation
to build on, a stage
for support
There is a point
for each season of our lives
Earth, water, air, fire
It is my compass I carry
for direction
I touch it when I am tongue-tied
or unable to believe

This ring is white like snow
and scratched with your tracks
It is the snow banked
in the eaves of my hand
Unlike the snow
it does not melt
or disappear like your kiss
on a zero day

This ring is a treasure I bury
in my fist, a flame
at the base of the shortest candle
At night it is the light
I leave on for you

Elements

for Cathy

It was so easy
to want so much:
your voice traveling the fibers
of the air, smooth and deep,
even with your cold,
guides me over treacherous rock,
through the night, through even more dangerous
disappointment to the next hour
of meeting.

* * *

I have made no resolutions
for the new year.
Instead, I will be like moisture
in the air. If the temperature
is right, I will be snow.
If wind is there,
I will be clouds.
If the clouds move on,
I will be the sun
shining through.

* * *

The face in the fire is not yours:
the woman is foreign.
She sits behind the wheel of a car
on a steep driveway.
Her eyes are blue spires
that reach toward me.
I am impaled.
I lean through the window,

kiss her.
The car rolls slowly in reverse.
The woman in the back seat
calls your name.

* * *

On each hand you wear
a bright ring:
circles of words, languages
you have spoken.
They could be segments
of chains
wandered free from the tribe,
cousins to the delicate links
that thread along your neck.
They are the stars
gleaming on dark water,
grains of gold
separated from the soil.

At my touch
the chain warms.
Strong, it has the memory
of string. It loops
on my finger,
shapes boundaries
against my hand.

It burns
like the ring
I no longer wear,
will always wear.

These faded blue

flowers
on the sheet
this Sunday

morning light
this house
still as though

you were off
in the shower or
had run out

for breakfast
milk
my hand

smooths
the wrinkles
as I make

the bed
with such easy
motion

would I
bring you
back

Writing in the House Where Everyone Sleeps

The unknown bird outside continues
to unwind its vocal spring

into these city-silent hours.
You are long gone to bed,

the blue of your nightgown floating
from this room like a daytime moon.

The children dream downstairs.
Even Rorschach the cat has quit whirring

and lies like a fur spill by the door.
In this black and white room

the second hand on the electric clock
still whips by at its hungry pace

though no one cares.
If I close my eyes

I could slip into sleep dark
as the underside of a bat's wing

where words come to me
like small moons freckling

the sky randomly with light
and I awake

to a sentence beginning
in the word *blue*

How I Imagine You Greet Me At the Airport

I trudge through the accordian tube,
the carpeted chute that returns
me from the sky to earth, that corridor
where each passenger thinks
of who is waiting, who is not.
I am thinking that you will be
standing somewhere nearly out of sight,
behind a man twice your size or an infant
whose squawling makes us all avert
our eyes. It is your eyes I see
first, even from this far, and then
your hands, or the full pockets
of your green parka where your hands
sleep. You approach me
tipped at a slight right angle
as I search for you
like a detail from a curious dream.
At this point, two welcomes
are possible:

in the first, we touch
some way, hand to arm, arm
to shoulder, breast against breast.
Perhaps your hair crosses
over my cheek or my cheek
brushes your ear. It is even possible
to kiss. Stranger things have happened
in midwestern airports. You lift
the backpack I carry to your own arm
and we turn toward the car.

In version two, you approach
grinning, as I do. Your hands
stay in their safe homes, mine grip

the handles of my bag like bird feet
on twigs. You say, *Hello,*
like a woman answering the phone.
I talk fast on my end, hand you
my backpack obese with books.
We move toward the terminal,
in stride, remarking on the nature
of wind in this place.

in separate cities

Ritual: Downtown Bar

without stories, a woman is lost
—Carol P. Christ, *Diving Deep and Surfacing*

Her grandmother died because the river took her house,
this woman who lived twenty years alone. Water moved
into the drowsy Missouri town, and when it left, there
was nothing left. In the same spot, the government
wheeled in a trailer, metal file for her life. No
plants survived, no china, no grandfather clock, long
hand missing. She could not dream in air conditioning.
No fire snapped in the panelled room. When the river
climbed its banks next spring, she was gone.

* * *

She lives with a man who welds ships. She wields words
like a torch. Together they have crossed the west,
crossed the law, crossed their lives. When they lie
together, they settle quiet as the small house. She
writes him letters in her sleep, asking if he smells
the salt air, what he has done with the small change
of her days, if he has watched the laundry signaling
from the line. He responds, fragments of breath
clouding the glass.

* * *

Her sister loves to wear ties—madras plaids, smooth
silks, knits—but especially the ones curled in paisley,
narrow as the ribbons she once wore in her hair. And
subtle colors, the blue and brown harmony of earth. In
the concrete building where she works, the rooms swarm with
men in ties—lightning bolts, angular rainbows, regimental
stripes. They weave a plot she is not part of, knots looped
so tight there is no space for air.

* * *

41

and, that spring I fell in love with a student.
Ohio changed. In the evening, the fields held
light longer than they ever had before. Old
farmhouses glowed bronze from within. I was never
in a hurry to be anywhere. All this I wrote in a
journal. Words escaped from nailed crates, stepped
boldly into phone booths, called me collect.
But I had no one to call. People said to fear the
things I felt. So we did not talk much, she and I,
and now in separate cities we are silent.

The Fragrant Shape of Petals

for Aunt Phyllis

Leaping from the paper, the gigantic yellow flowers
blossom loudly on the wall of my aunt's sunny kitchen,
immersing us in perpetual summer gardens.
I seem like tiny Alice, half-expecting
that Cheshire grin to peer from behind their leaves.
The round glass table reflects
the fragrant shape of petals,
a lily pond swimming below our hands.
If I look hard into the glass
I fall back to the past: I am a child awaking
to a corridor flooded with the smell of bacon,
hubbub in this kitchen at its end.
I unpack items crisp and folded (usually
blue) from my suitcase.
Out in the pool, rubber seahorses bob
nonchalantly, undisturbed
by their green and purple spots.
At night, I will swim there, teeth chattering,
with spots of my own, mesmerized
by the eerie glow of the lightning bug-like
underwater light. I pretend to be on Mars.
Before the pool came, a wooden teeter-totter
blasted all the cousins to the moon (and obviously back),
this one clad in a starched white shirt
stenciled with the license plates of our forty-eight states.
Somewhere I hear my father's voice declaring,
Bea, that will never fit in the trunk!
and I see my brother, shaped like Tweedledee,
his finger held out straight before his nose
like a misplaced rudder,
take his first steps for my aunt.
For hours he navigated through those yellow flowers
afraid that to stop meant permanent drydock.

43

I, too, return to these flowers,
alone now. They are bright beads
on the abacus of memory, yellow bloom
flourishing still.

Just Like In The Movies

for Edna Clemans

I drive into town down this two lane street,
the brick halls of the university
indifferent to my approach. I note how little
has changed. More leaves than students
collect on the lawns, their bright reds and yellows
like ski jackets on a white slope.
The first frost has come.
We see our breath in the air.

In the red house on Biddle Street
I drink tea with an old friend.
She has given up smoking,
I have given up meat. We both
have given up letters.
We tell what has happened to the people
we know—who's been published,
who's been divorced.
We share interests in photography
and rummage through flea markets
like squirrels searching
for nuts. Her orange cat has no more use
for me now than he did then.

We go for lunch to the local pizzaria
and argue over the check. She pays,
though I ate the most. We drive
down Main Street past the rambling grey house
where I used to live. Now it is green,
and the store next door sells bicycles,
roller skates, and health food.
My friend says the owner no longer wears
the pyramid on her head. I wonder
if it is because winter nears

and this town is too cold
without a hat. We pass the vacant lot
where last year the Ross Hotel
burned to the ground.
They say it was arson.

Back in the house, after one more cup of tea,
we say goodbye. I have brought
my old Kansas license plate for her collection
on the garage wall. She gives me an ERA button
from the 1972 Democratic Convention,
and a buckeye for my pocket
to keep arthritis away.
She walks me to my car, waves
as I back into the street.
I close my fist tight
around the warm hard buckeye,
grin like a runner
just breaking the tape.

Trimming the Tree

for Celia

Two women are alone in a room.
What is possible between them
and who will record it?

—Louise Bernikow

It is time again to do the tree,
to perform the ritual of hanging gold
balls, cloth angels, china bells
dated 1975, 1976, 1977 and odd, rare symbols
shaped by the hands of friends.
We step carefully among the cardboard boxes,
reach into nests of shredded newsprint,
tissue paper, and wads of napkins
in search of something small, something
solid, some tinkle of glass.

Candles burn around the room—
musk, vanilla, and overpowering cranberry.
It is too warm for early December,
so I build no fire. We drink
mugs of blackberry tea. Lights on the tree
glow lazily, their greens, blues, reds
doorknobs to memory. I think
of a dream I had last night:
you and I as lovers wandering a large city,
struggling to negotiate the intricacies
of unfamiliar interstates. I wait
for you in a restaurant. You never show up.
The sharp needle of the fir pricks my hand
as I hang a silver star on a low branch.

Earlier we sat on the couch talking:
your life with your father, your husband's
father's death at his own hand, my past

47

lovers, my fall trip through the east.
Over enchiladas at La Palma's, we tell
how hard it is to say goodbye.
I dangle a yellow bird in a cave of the tree
and remember that in the morning
you will be gone.

I have never trimmed the tree alone.
The hands of my lovers have always laced
among the branches with mine.
Now in distant towns, these women
live new lives, trim their own trees.
Even you have moved far north,
but tonight you are here.
We drank wine together before they came;
we do it now when they are gone.
You are each season of my life:
easy autumn after summer's frantic
heat, the snow that brings
the spring to green. Alone with you
in this room tonight, I share
what centuries of women too often leave unsaid.
You give me gifts that need no wrap, no reasons.

Tonight the sky

is a black eye. The bruised
veins grow plump,
clotting with blood, the surface

purple as royal birth.
Too full, the canals flood,
soak into the dark,
disappear. Tonight I am filled

with my own life.
It spills out, lengthens

in deep cuts, painful and alive,
uncontrollable as the bruise
below my left knee.

Even the air
holds its breath, unsure

of what comes next.

The cars on the streets I walk
talk to each other
in monosyllabic lights. They say

the same word again
and again, a sentence of one word

racing from the bluegrass state
to Kansas. The word is *dream,*

fruit, or perhaps *sleep.*
The word could be your name, the bud

on the tree too frail
to contain the April bloom,

the single star that springs
from this morning sky.

How we drive each other

to words, you and I,
letters shuffling between our cities

like commuter trains
I feel language rooting

in my fingertips,
sentences necessary as blood

I hear you in an unlit corner
speaking words

I recite as I travel home
I send back words red

as the dozen roses he might send,
green as Nebraska that spring

I send words explosive
as seeds,

unsure as the rabbit
cornered by two hounds

You return words to me:
neon signs

in the night,
the extra quilt I fling

on the bed
Your words fill

this house, splashing out
like balloons

51

when I open the mail
I see syllables line up

like freeway traffic,
jockey in and out

the motor hums
in my Smith-Corona 7000

As the light turns yellow
I race through

In Exchange

for Carol

Christmas eve and still they come.
The mail slot coughs up cards
from Chicago, Toledo, Oakland.
I flip through return addresses.
Yours leaps up like the swift deer
leaving only tracks in snow,
a white rectangle among red
and holly green squares.
It is the first I open.

You write me a poem
about postcards, about love
scrawled in hurried words
on the backs of unlikely photos
from yet more unlikely spot.
We are all temporary,
and you know it.

This year we have abandoned
our towns, a couple of bandits
trying not to look back.
We mail letters, appearing
inconspicuous, disguised
as mundane correspondence, news
from the girl next door.
What we send are silver rings,
the family's last jewel, a loaf
of just-baked bread, a basket
with fruit. You write,
I'm lonely.

Your letters bring you close as this fire
I write beside now. A page drops

on my lap like a scarf
you left behind. I read the pattern,
search the design: here,
an upstairs room in your house in Tulsa.
With the light out, we honor
the power of language, speak
of the words that save us
in the dark. Your letter brings
a solstice gift, a compass,
a celebration of interiors,
yours and my own.
It opens my life, a knife
slicing across my thumb.
My body starts. I know
I am alive.

Intercepted Message

    for Adrienne Rich

send something back, you wrote
If you can read and understand this poem
send something back

For days I have been thinking
what to send
from this horizontal state lost
between the coasts:

light   the magnetic fire
that burns October trees

this ash, this sycamore
sparks flick their way inside
the window glass

the light that rises, blooming
in hues we have no name for
female color, strata
of deep canyons, clay
of ancient pots,

stretching tendrils, fissures
in the sky's crust at dusk

fossil   from these Flint Hills
proof of our simpler past, a question
always asking itself anew

something to trust with your fingertips
a heartbeat caught mid-rock

sunflowers   out here
they stand
like Amazons above the wheat
their faces alert
their spear-tipped petals truer
than gold

when the tornado takes the house
the barn, the father
and the cow
sunflowers stay on
to hold down the land

I send you words:

seeds
an imprint on this transitory page
something to carry in the dark, something
that will not fail

where our lives intersect

Where We Are Going, Where We Have Been

for Lisel Mueller

We cannot say where our lives intersect,
yours and mine, myself and the pasts
that I am, the histories you are.
If we examine an old photograph,
my grandmother's wealthy cousin is the bystander
staring on from the upper left, behind
the slatted park bench, as your unknown foremother
snaps the shutter, so pleased with the gathering.
Life boomerangs like that.
You teach the older sister of my best friend's
first husband. Tomorrow I discover how
often we make the same story.

There are those things we must unlearn
to survive: how to give and not take, how to act
the lady, how to be seen and not heard.
We remember the trusted voice of instruction,
how we were told it would be, how different
it is. We learn promise is not fact.
What we count on is neither memory
nor dream. We construct both as we go.

We are strangers. And then we are not.
Something intimate weighs in the handshake,
the way the light shapes a pond of your green ring.
Some secret lurks in the Siamese shadows
we cast, something unlikely we might never guess.
It has already occurred. It has yet
to happen. It remains obsolete
or uninvented. It will seek
the sun. It will deny such connection.

For Susan, turning thirty

this November, the brown leaves
will sweep across empty intersections
in these early morning hours
as they have for years, as they did
when we waited for schoolbuses, pumpkin
and cider in the air, or on those southern
mountain mornings when frost needled our paths
to the main road.

Last night, when I said I had known you
for twenty-five years, I grew older
than our first grade teacher, lumbering
through the chalk-filled sunlit room in white
anklets and oxfords. The twins,
an English teacher called us, as we circled
in identical orbits, mine always with
imperfections, just slightly off-course.
I looked in mirrors hoping
you would look back:
I was Castor, you Pollux.

Years later, you are still
the protagonist in my dreams:
your face replaces that of the woman
I stand next to, you sit in my classroom,
you are with me in blizzards, car wrecks,
at the opposite end of the green felt table
in smoke-filled rooms.
We are customers watching
a grocer weigh bologna, and I turn
to ask you, *Are rock lyrics poetry?*
If you are not there
I am searching.

We are each other
even now: I feel my hand
lift a glass at your table,
the dolls I buy are for your daughters.
I have fled to Kansas and you have moved
into my territory, a few houses
from my house. The heavens spread
between us. Now we are differences:
our choice of partners, the way
we dress, the books that change
our lives. I could not write this poem
for myself, turned thirty
in September. Once again,
it is for you, it is for me.

When it happens

I will be in a car
and the day will be washwater grey
and hanging on the western
horizon, rags of violet and blue
several cars already beam their lights on
jousting with night
a small plane scouts overhead, perhaps
checking for speeders
there will be flecks of snow
on the fields below
the trees, in naked chorus
outlined in white
the water in the pond
is not yet frozen

In the dream
a metallic green Corvair
and I am with Susan
my friend for life
we travel through
a neat Ohio town
sharing an important secret
we lean toward each other
not yet twenty-three
I am the driver
suddenly the windshield
splatters with water
I wake up somewhere else

That prophecy, however
has proven false
the Corvair expired
in a Christmas blizzard
Susan married, has children

doesn't leave home much anymore
and I am ten years older
still each time I skid
toward the guard rail
on a winter highway
feel a tire give up beneath me
or see headlights approach
my side of the road
I think of Susan
sitting with her daughters
by the kitchen window
and wonder how soon before she hears
the shattering of glass

The Back Fence

This is traditionally the place
for gathering:
heavy women in cotton print
dresses, thin women in
halter tops
arranging appointments,
exchanging lives,
men in coarse laughter
asking favors.
Even the dogs poke their noses
through the boards.
And the setting is right:
one brick house, one white house,
a clothes pole and swing set
in my yard, a picnic table
in yours.
The grass always needs
cutting, the white pickets
another coat of paint.
We stand here often,
wrapped in the hot Kansas
afternoon, discussing the horror
of wallpaper or
playing tennis with a hangover.
Later, you water tomatoes,
I bring the clothes in, singing.
We cross the fence
to fix lawnmowers
or drinks.
I cling to the habit
of this fence,
on its points I hang
my day.
We have been here in other times,

touched our hands to the rough wood,
chipped white paint with our nails.
Perhaps, then, it was
stone, and our arms rubbed
smooth on its worn ledge,
or barbed wire,
and we did not touch it
at all.

Legacy

She kept all these things
put away in a black strongbox:
her birth certificate; his honorable
discharge from the army in 1919.
Under conduct, it says *Excellent.*
He was a bookkeeper. Back home
his precise script marks name
after name on the payroll, a dark
delicate line crossing off those swallowed up
in the black currents of the shaft;
a pistol, which would be stolen
years later, when she would not know;
a gold watch chain, its links intricate,
frail as the years of their lives;
his certificate of death.
In 1922 the funeral cost
one hundred twenty dollars.
She was twenty-three years old,
two daughters at home, another
swimming in the womb;
a letter beginning
Dearest wife . . . typed,
dated July 1922, asking if she got
the two dollars he sent from Michigan,
inquiring politely as to her health.
His eyes were blue, like my own
I am sure, full of light
like shallow water, his hair
brown, perhaps sandy in sunshine,
his height five foot seven and a half.
I always saw him taller
than my father.
When I saw the picture,
he was already in the coffin,

flag-draped, guarded by gladiola
and iris (morbid, my mother always said)
in a chapel barely large enough
to hold my questions, still unasked.
All those years I thought
he drowned off the unimportant shoals
of the muddy Kanawha, a few minutes
from home, on a day just like any other
except for this one detail.
Now I discover it was a mistake.
In Lake Superior, miles from our hard-rock
mountains, a friend struggling to get through
to the opening of air wrestled him down,
cramps like lead weights tied to his legs.
She never remarried.
I never heard her say his name
or saw her enter water more than waist deep.
My mother is named
for the other man's wife.

Crawlspace

for Carol Konek

What I am trying to say
is that the details

do not matter:
that it was a gusty February

afternoon, unusually
warm, that the room

had little sunlight
or why we were both there

in my eyes you found
the sloping shaft

my hands struggling
with the beams:

your arm lightly
around me, my head

against you, the passage
I slip through

The First Colby Poem

for Sharon Hixon

Until last week you were only a voice
on the phone, a mailing address
in western Kansas, a deadline
to dread. I have been in your town
a week now, and on this snowy Saturday
afternoon, I swing my van
into the tracks in your driveway
hoping you are home.

You open the back door as my finger
points toward the doorbell,
invite me into a kitchen
smelling of cookies and fresh clothes.
One son sits in pajamas
before the t.v. Your husband
takes my coat. I plop on the couch
like we are high school best friends,
as if I had been dropping in
for years.

We talk about my students, your friends,
why so many folks return
to Colby, Kansas. You ask
if I have seen the museum yet
or been to the library. I praise
the Blakesley Hotel, steam radiators
clanking into the night, glass
pitchers with ice beside the bed,
the bath with immaculate white tiles.

I slip back to childhood
where good friends joined their blood

with the prick of a pin, shiver
when I think where some of us
are now. I am a woman
from places you may never know.

These seven days we have shared
dinners, poems, popcorn
at midnight when the rest of the house
slept. You are my bookmark
in this town, my footnote to the text.
Later we will recount these days,
our lives bleeding together in the wash,
how we were strangers
the first time our hands clasped.

City Park: March Sunday

They gather slowly; it is the first
time this year for some, the first time
in twenty years for others.
Tossing balls in high arcs, bringing
beagles on chains, sharing banana splits
from Baskin-Robbins, their numbers
increase. Now, small boys and fathers
must be removed diplomatically
from the diamond. Wooden bats
smack together between the plops
dropping into leather pockets.

An audience of kites collects,
quarrels overhead. Ones and twos,
counted off, the teams form:
twos take the field. Third base,
whose hand was minced by a vegetable
grinder earlier in the week, cannot
wear a glove. Center field and second
huddle together, jackets flapping,
lighting cigarettes. The catcher hunts
for home plate. The pitcher smooths the mound
with bare feet.

Batters take the plate: some swing
like limbs in the Kansas wind, back
and forth, in a rustle of words;
for others, balls scurry through
the dirt, over frantic hands and feet;
some sail it kite-high, off toward
the Safeway, then watch a glove
hug it close. Dust blows
applause in the face of the next batter

71

who swings, looks straight
at the gold medal of sun, starts
to run as the runner comes home.

Making Sense Of It All

You are perplexed, you say, by the movie,
a story whose pieces seem mismatched
socks, several puzzles
all dumped in one box.
It will take you days to sort them out.

We drive home beneath a sky
anxious with rain, the sweet smell
imminent in the air. I am thinking
of the movie, too, of the men in white
sprinting like gulls on the water's edge,
feet slapping the skin of the waves.
We plunge into an intersection,
the streetlights mirrored moons in our wake.
I see the men, hoisted like sacks
to the shoulders of their athletic friends,
oblivious to the weight, the shouts of the crowd.
Thunder leaps the hurdles down the dark lane.

We both want this storm, its damp breath
heaving across us as we sleep, its million toes
tapping, all stepping up for the same race.
Upstairs, where you sleep now, a door
bangs shut like a starting gun:
I feel my spikes bite down on the dirt track,
bite down, bite down, and I turn
my glance to see you,
the tape snapping like lightning
against the numbers on your chest.

Mowing

On a day when the clouds keep arguing
rain, then sun, I leave the slashed damp grass
in orderly trails north and south,
careful to avoid the rusty knife, clear glass
beer bottle, styrofoam cup that would
shred up, a summer blizzard
in the indecisive air. I mow in long rows,
a rectangle munching in on itself.
Near the Rose of Sharon you first
burst through my logical thought,
no more than a small sharp imprint,
a number on the page. I continue
itemizing groceries along the garage,
turn right at the sycamore where I catch
you balancing just inside the corner
of my left eye. You are grinning
and *peanut butter* is what I hear
you say. By the time I make two sweeps
past the ash, you have parked your car
in the middle of the conversation
I contemplate with the Dean. You want to know
if I have time to go for ice cream.
I, of course, say *yes*
and keep mowing, noticing how the sky
puffs up like hot air balloons.
Crossing into the back yard,
between the apple and the pin oak,
I find you asleep, stretched
full length across my afternoon
trip downtown. We both know you are impossible
to wake. The mower chokes, strangled
by dandelion stems. Raindrops
parachute onto my hands.

Gift

In this room, carpet too white
for snow, we make a field.

Our words prolong the light.
Your blue eyes are roses that grow

here, their leaves blades that sharpen
with the night.

Now I want to ask you
to look for the center, how the petals

pull themselves back, how they
have denied thorns. Their roots

bind my heart.
I want to clip them at the bone,

watch them
unfold in my hand.

Sometimes like birds

your hands light
on the branches
inside my skin
their strong hearts
beat language
the secret of stark trees
their feathers brush
night from open windows

your hands open
a canyon
holding
nuggets in deep cracks

your hands wrap me
in the vines of sleep
fingers like leaves
wandering

my body
flows to your hands
a ball of twine
unwinding
turns to sand

your fingers make bright threads
weaving, weaving
turquoise, carnelian, emerald
the cloth with no border
no end to color

in the mirror
of your hands
light and shade

hands and feet
touching
the house and the land
those places
we live

Touching Me As Only You Can

Crab-like, I hunker in the squat aluminum chair
warmed by the sun, chilled by the wind

on cliffs that fringe the Pacific
my toes poke the loose sand

I am unable to predict
which wave will crest, then crash

which will scoot in
unnoticed, unannounced

on the horizon boats appear
lost in dreams, swimmers lie exposed

on opposite rocks
behind me stalking gulls disagree

like aunts sorting through old photos
some troop off, always it seems

in twos, skimming haphazardly
over the water

their sudden shadows cross me
as the gulls cross overhead

Fear

for Beth Alexander

you say you have it
and I understand
it is hearing
a bone start
to break, a heart

waiting to stop
it is waking
to find a sharp man
his body
pointed at you

it is being a woman
with sons
or a woman without
it is risking
with me

a poem about what you did
when it came
it is what I know
as I struggle toward
this poem for you

Somewhere Just Beyond

Be happy, my daughter.
You think I have magic powers,
others call it love.
I tell you it is the will
to survive, in you, in the earth.
Your story does not end
with the wedding dance, it goes on.

—Lisel Mueller

I transport the pot of tulips
to the back yard,
their shrivelled sunset blossoms
resting on green stalks,
plant them in a shallow pit
from which, next spring, they will burn
like the Phoenix. When their flames
open to the air I will remember you, awaiting
resurrection in your narrow hospital bed,
tan blanket drifted over you
like desert sand, your knees shifting
dunes, the oasis
somewhere just beyond.

The wind stirs unexpectedly
in this blank place
where time sleeps like an exhausted child.
You wander in the storm
behind your eyes.
Faces impose like the Sphinx
and riddles are the only conversation.
Sand settles in your veins. You sink
to the floor. Inside your head
slaves begin a pyramid. Tons of rock
drag over your skull.

Each day you study the sand,
its senseless movement, its increasing
weight. You learn how to change
these grains to flights of snow,
to a spring thaw flooding
the dry room. You sip
from these fresh pools and lift
up your hands. Your mouth
sounds the words
after this, after this.

Women Who Cook

When, this incredible thing, the principal of the junior high,
surprised by a blast from an M-1A rifle, slumps
a few feet from his office door, or the woman
out jogging in the Saturday morning snow, jubilant
as confetti, gets beaten and raped, or the son
does not recover from the ache in his side, we are left,
hands fumbling in pockets for more
than just words.

The doorbell rings. A woman appears, offering
an aluminum pan wrapped in foil. *I wanted to make something
chocolate,* she says, *but there isn't anything chocolate
I can make really well.* A later hour, another ring:
She made you these rolls, he says, extending the sack
like a drowned cat. Still later, a glass dish
held out like a crystal ball: *We had this extra ham,*
she says. *We thought you could use it now.*

I remember February's worst blizzard since 1912
when my grandmother, who made cornbread when Stevie's mother
did not return from the trip and blackberry cobbler
when Earle stayed down in the mine, chose
to die. A four wheel drive took the body
and brought beans. Friends plowed through snow
with potato salad and stew. Wherever I turned,
I was handed a dish. My hands steamed for days.

Some of us women still bake, she says, *when we don't know
what else to do.* I take the butterscotch pie, meringue
frothy and deep as that February snow, and turn toward the kitchen,
thinking of women who turn on their stoves, take down their bowls.
I lift this gift, this tangible sorrow, to the shelf.
Right now, in this town, a woman beats eggs, each stroke
a blow against something out there, something
only a neighbor away.

82

February Letter

The night you left, the first night
of an already long December, snow wrapped
the house in flannel bandages.
What we had not said
drifted in the corners of every room.

We've met since then in dreams,
you in your faded red soccer uniform,
towel tucked into your shorts like a loincloth,
making up songs about groundhogs
or talking about bad laws and basketball.
Did I think you would come
in garments of white light?

Yesterday I cleaned off my desk,
anticipating the next semester's clutter,
and under a year old stack
of mail, your handwriting trailed
across the page.

A note from you lies
folded like a limp rag, a polishing
cloth put away. When I unfold
the creases and see your name
in boldface type, you charge the air.

The hands of the women

I love sometimes
swing like axes in the air

the timber of words
colliding

crashing to the ground
often their hands

dress in intricate rings
labyrinths of silver and gold

lines binding their lives
in place

the stones buttons
to the heart

moving
they make shapes

bowls come from the womb
of their hands

my grandmother's hands
were the first hands

I watched snapping
beans

hanging clothes
on the frozen rope

mending socks
the veins of her hands

stood up strong
as her life

blue as her eyes
the hands of these women

web the room
each hand a map

a guide
some highway to follow

their hands peel back
the skin of night

sometimes their hands
hold mine

A few of the publications of
THE NAIAD PRESS, INC.
P.O. Box 10543 • Tallahassee, Florida 32302
Mail orders welcome. Please include 15% postage.

THE LOVE OF GOOD WOMEN by Isabel Miller. 224 pp. Long-awaited new novel by the author of the beloved *Patience and Sarah.*   ISBN 0-930044-81-9 $8.95

THE HOUSE AT PELHAM FALLS by Brenda Weathers. 240 pp. Suspenseful Lesbian ghost story.   ISBN 0-930044-79-7   7.95

HOME IN YOUR HANDS by Lee Lynch. 240 pp. More stories from the author of *Old Dyke Tales.*   ISBN 0-930044-80-0   7.95

EACH HAND A MAP by Anita Skeen. 112 pp. Real-life poems that touch us all.   ISBN 0-930044-82-7   6.95

SURPLUS by Sylvia Stevenson. 342 pp. A classic early Lesbian novel.   ISBN 0-930044-78-9   7.95

PEMBROKE PARK by Michelle Martin. 256 pp. Derring-do and daring romance in Regency England.
                  ISBN 0-930044-77-0   7.95

THE LONG TRAIL by Penny Hayes. 248 pp. Vivid adventures of two women in love in the old west.   ISBN 0-930044-76-2   8.95

HORIZON OF THE HEART by Shelley Smith. 192 pp. Sizzling romance in summertime New England.
                  ISBN 0-930044-75-4   7.95

AN EMERGENCE OF GREEN by Katherine V. Forrest. 288 pp. Powerful novel of sexual discovery.   ISBN 0-930044-69-X   8.95

THE LESBIAN PERIODICALS INDEX edited by Claire Potter. 432 pp. Author and subject index.
                  ISBN 0-930044-74-6   29.95

DESERT OF THE HEART by Jane Rule. 224 pp. A classic; basis for the movie *Desert Hearts.*   ISBN 0-930044-73-8   7.95

SPRING FORWARD/FALL BACK by Sheila Ortiz Taylor. 288 pp. Literary novel of timeless love.   ISBN 0-930044-70-3   7.95

FOR KEEPS by Elisabeth Nonas. 144 pp. Contemporary novel about losing and finding love.   ISBN 0-930044-71-1   7.95

TORCHLIGHT TO VALHALLA by Gale Wilhelm. 128 pp. Classic novel by a great Lesbian writer.   ISBN 0-930044-68-1   7.95

LESBIAN NUNS: BREAKING SILENCE edited by Rosemary Curb and Nancy Manahan. 432 pp. Unprecedented autobiographies of religious life.   ISBN 0-930044-62-2   9.95

THE SWASHBUCKLER by Lee Lynch. 288 pp. Colorful novel set in Greenwich Village in the sixties.   ISBN 0-930044-66-5   7.95

MISFORTUNE'S FRIEND by Sarah Aldridge. 320 pp. Historical Lesbian novel set on two continents.
                  ISBN 0-930044-67-3   7.95

A STUDIO OF ONE'S OWN by Ann Stokes. Edited by
Dolores Klaich. 128 pp. Autobiography. ISBN 0-930044-64-9   7.95

SEX VARIANT WOMEN IN LITERATURE by Jeannette
Howard Foster. 448 pp. Literary history. ISBN 0-930044-65-7   8.95

A HOT-EYED MODERATE by Jane Rule. 252 pp. Hard-hitting
essays on gay life; writing; art.   ISBN 0-930044-57-6   7.95

INLAND PASSAGE AND OTHER STORIES by Jane Rule.
288 pp. Wide-ranging new collection.   ISBN 0-930044-56-8   7.95

WE TOO ARE DRIFTING by Gale Wilhelm. 128 pp. Timeless
Lesbian novel, a masterpiece.   ISBN 0-930044-61-4   6.95

AMATEUR CITY by Katherine V. Forrest. 224 pp. A Kate
Delafield mystery. First in a series.   ISBN 0-930044-55-X   7.95

THE SOPHIE HOROWITZ STORY by Sarah Schulman. 176
pp. Engaging novel of madcap intrigue.   ISBN 0-930044-54-1   7.95

THE BURNTON WIDOWS by Vicki P. McConnell. 272 pp. A
Nyla Wade mystery, second in the series. ISBN 0-930044-52-5   7.95

OLD DYKE TALES by Lee Lynch. 224 pp. Extraordinary
stories of our diverse Lesbian lives.   ISBN 0-930044-51-7   7.95

DAUGHTERS OF A CORAL DAWN by Katherine V. Forrest.
240 pp. Novel set in a Lesbian new world.ISBN 0-930044-50-9   7.95

THE PRICE OF SALT by Claire Morgan. 288 pp. A milestone
novel, a beloved classic.   ISBN 0-930044-49-5   8.95

AGAINST THE SEASON by Jane Rule. 224 pp. Luminous,
complex novel of interrelationships.   ISBN 0-930044-48-7   7.95

LOVERS IN THE PRESENT AFTERNOON by Kathleen
Fleming. 288 pp. A novel about recovery and growth.
                                         ISBN 0-930044-46-0   8.50

TOOTHPICK HOUSE by Lee Lynch. 264 pp. Love between
two Lesbians of different classes.   ISBN 0-930044-45-2   7.95

MADAME AURORA by Sarah Aldridge. 256 pp. Historical
novel featuring a charismatic "seer."   ISBN 0-930044-44-4   7.95

CURIOUS WINE by Katherine V. Forrest. 176 pp. Passionate
Lesbian love story, a best-seller.   ISBN 0-930044-43-6   7.95

BLACK LESBIAN IN WHITE AMERICA by Anita Cornwell.
141 pp. Stories, essays, autobiography. ISBN 0-930044-41-X   7.50

CONTRACT WITH THE WORLD by Jane Rule. 340 pp.
Powerful, panoramic novel of gay life.   ISBN 0-930044-28-2   7.95

YANTRAS OF WOMANLOVE by Tee A. Corinne. 64 pp.
Photographs by the noted Lesbian photographer.
                                         ISBN 0-930044-30-4   6.95

MRS. PORTER'S LETTER by Vicki P. McConnell. 224 pp.
The first Nyla Wade mystery.   ISBN 0-930044-29-0   7.95

TO THE CLEVELAND STATION by Carol Anne Douglas.
192 pp. Interracial Lesbian love story. ISBN 0-930044-27-4   6.95

THE NESTING PLACE by Sarah Aldridge. 224 pp. Historical novel, a three-woman triangle. ISBN 0-930044-26-6   7.95

THIS IS NOT FOR YOU by Jane Rule. 284 pp. A letter to a beloved is also an intricate novel. ISBN 0-930044-25-8   7.95

FAULTLINE by Sheila Ortiz Taylor. 140 pp. Warm, funny, literate story of a startling family. ISBN 0-930044-24-X   6.95

THE LESBIAN IN LITERATURE by Barbara Grier. 3d ed. Foreword by Maida Tilchen. 240 pp. A comprehensive bibliography. Literary ratings; rare photographs.
ISBN 0-930044-23-1   7.95

ANNA'S COUNTRY by Elizabeth Lang. 208 pp. A woman finds her Lesbian identity. ISBN 0-930044-19-3   6.95

PRISM by Valerie Taylor. 158 pp. A love affair between two women in their sixties. ISBN 0-930044-18-5   6.95

BLACK LESBIANS: AN ANNOTATED BIBLIOGRAPHY compiled by J.R. Roberts. Foreword by Barbara Smith. 112 pp. Award winning bibliography. ISBN 0-930044-21-5   5.95

THE MARQUISE AND THE NOVICE by Victoria Ramstetter. 108 pp. A Lesbian Gothic novel. ISBN 0-930044-16-9   4.95

LABIAFLOWERS by Tee A. Corinne. 40 pp. Drawings by the noted artist/photographer. ISBN 0-930044-20-7   3.95

OUTLANDER by Jane Rule. 207 pp. Short stories and essays by one of our finest writers. ISBN 0-930044-17-7   6.95

SAPPHISTRY: THE BOOK OF LESBIAN SEXUALITY by Pat Califia. 2d edition, revised. 195 pp. ISBN 0-930044-47-9   7.95

ALL TRUE LOVERS by Sarah Aldridge. 292 pp. Romantic novel set in the 1930s and 1940s. ISBN 0-930044-10-X   7.95

A WOMAN APPEARED TO ME by Renee Vivien. 65 pp. A classic; translation by Jeannette H. Foster.
ISBN 0-930044-06-1   5.00

CYTHEREA'S BREATH by Sarah Aldridge. 240 pp. Women first entering medicine and the law: a novel.
ISBN 0-930044-02-9   6.95

TOTTIE by Sarah Aldridge. 181 pp. Lesbian romance in the turmoil of the sixties. ISBN 0-930044-01-0   6.95

THE LATECOMER by Sarah Aldridge. 107 pp. A delicate love story set in days gone by. ISBN 0-930044-00-2   5.00

ODD GIRL OUT by Ann Bannon   ISBN 0-930044-83-5   5.95
I AM A WOMAN by Ann Bannon.   ISBN 0-930044-84-3   5.95
WOMEN IN THE SHADOWS by Ann Bannon.
ISBN 0-930044-85-1   5.95
JOURNEY TO A WOMAN by Ann Bannon.
ISBN 0-930044-86-X   5.95
BEEBO BRINKER by Ann Bannon   ISBN 0-930044-87-8   5.95

Legendary novels written in the fifties and sixties,
set in the gay mecca of Greenwich Village.

VOLUTE BOOKS